Wild, Wet, and Windy!

Written by Claire Owen

My name is Tom. I live in
Fort Worth, Texas, which is in
"Tornado Alley." Can you guess
which states of the U.S. are
the wettest? … the windiest?
… the wildest? What is the
wildest weather that you have
ever experienced?

Contents

Wherever you see me, you'll find activities to try and questions to answer.

Whatever the Weather

What is the weather like in the United States? The answer, of course, is that it varies from place to place, from season to season, from day to day—and sometimes even from hour to hour! The weather in Alaska is very different from the weather in Florida or Hawaii. The weather is not likely to be the same at the top of the Rocky Mountains and in the California desert. Meteorologists record and study local weather patterns. This information helps them predict, or forecast, the coming weather.

These giant hailstones fell near Sitka, Kansas.

meteorologist   a scientist who studies weather, climate, and the atmosphere

4

Forecast High Temperatures

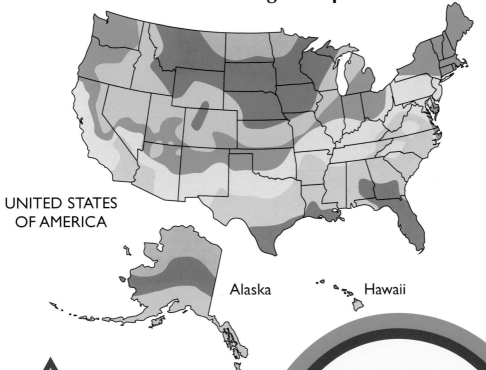

UNITED STATES
OF AMERICA

Alaska

Hawaii

KEY:

0s
10s
20s
30s
40s
50s
60s
70s
80s
90s

The map above shows a range of forecast maximum temperatures for a day in February. Was this an average, mild, or cool day in your state?

On the map, point to two places in different states that have a temperature difference of about—
- 10 degrees.
- 40 degrees.
- 60 degrees.

Wild Weather

Over the centuries, the United States has had its share
of the world's wildest weather! Every year, the country has
more tornadoes than any other region on Earth. Most of
these twisters occur in an area called "Tornado Alley,"
which includes parts of Texas, Oklahoma, Kansas, Colorado,
Nebraska, and Iowa. Sometimes tornadoes that form on land
travel over lakes or oceans and form waterspouts.

waterspout   a spinning column of water and spray

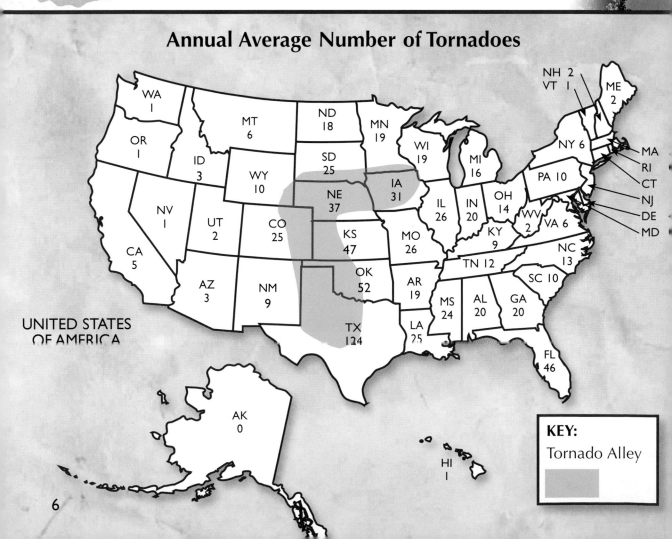

Annual Average Number of Tornadoes

WA 1
OR 1
MT 6
ND 18
MN 19
NH 2
VT 1
ME 2
ID 3
SD 25
WI 19
MI 16
NY 6
WY 10
NE 37
IA 31
PA 10
MA
RI
CT
NJ
DE
MD
NV 1
UT 2
CO 25
IL 26
IN 20
OH 14
WV 2
VA 6
KS 47
MO 26
KY 9
NC 13
CA 5
AZ 3
NM 9
OK 52
AR 19
TN 12
SC 10
MS 24
AL 20
GA 20
TX 124
LA 25
FL 46

UNITED STATES
OF AMERICA

AK 0

HI 1

KEY:
Tornado Alley

6

Tornadoes are between 300 and 2,000 feet wide and travel at speeds of 20 to 45 miles per hour. Although a tornado usually lasts only a few minutes, it can lift houses into the air and rip trees from the ground.

Which state is hit by the greatest number of tornadoes each year? Does that state also have the greatest average per 10,000 square miles? Why or why not?

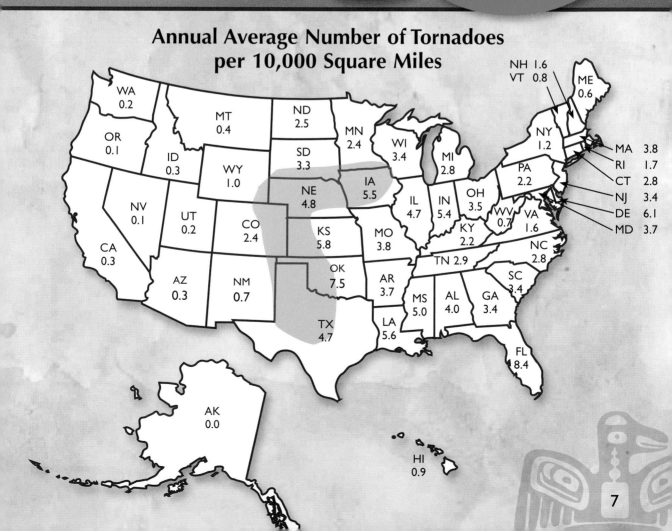

Annual Average Number of Tornadoes per 10,000 Square Miles

WA 0.2
OR 0.1
ID 0.3
MT 0.4
ND 2.5
SD 3.3
WY 1.0
MN 2.4
WI 3.4
MI 2.8
NY 1.2
NH 1.6
VT 0.8
ME 0.6
MA 3.8
RI 1.7
CT 2.8
NJ 3.4
DE 6.1
MD 3.7
PA 2.2
NV 0.1
UT 0.2
CO 2.4
NE 4.8
IA 5.5
IL 4.7
IN 5.4
OH 3.5
WV 0.7
VA 1.6
CA 0.3
AZ 0.3
NM 0.7
KS 5.8
MO 3.8
KY 2.2
NC 2.8
TN 2.9
SC 3.4
OK 7.5
AR 3.7
MS 5.0
AL 4.0
GA 3.4
TX 4.7
LA 5.6
FL 8.4
AK 0.0
HI 0.9

Terrifying Tornadoes

The most powerful and devastating tornado in the history of the United States occurred on March 18, 1925. The Great Tri-State Tornado traveled 219 miles in $3\frac{1}{2}$ hours, through Missouri, Illinois, and Indiana. The twister destroyed four towns and severely damaged six others. Altogether, about 15,000 homes were destroyed. Another raging record was set on April 3 and 4, 1974, when 148 tornadoes swept through southern and midwestern states in 21 hours.

Pick any two dates on these pages. Figure out the number of years, months, and days between those dates.

devastate   to ruin or destroy

Tornado Tales

- The first recorded U.S. tornado occurred on July 8, 1680, in Cambridge, Massachusetts.

- The world-record wind speed of 286 miles per hour was measured inside a tornado at Wichita Falls, Texas, on April 2, 1958.

- The number of tornadoes in the U.S. is about 20 times greater than in Britain. However, Britain averages one tornado every 2,856 square miles compared to one every 3,345 square miles in the U.S.

- The highest waterspout ever recorded was on May 16, 1898, off the coast of Australia. It was estimated to be 5,014 feet high.

In a Hurry

A hurricane is a tropical storm with strong winds that rotate at speeds of at least 74 miles per hour. Hurricanes form over the ocean but only where the water temperature is warmer than 80°F. These powerful storms are usually accompanied by rain, thunder, and lightning, and they can cause severe damage when they move from the sea to the land. When they reach shallow water, they can cause a rise in sea level called a *storm surge*.

Hurricanes usually last for about a week. High winds may destroy property, and heavy rains may cause flooding and mudslides.

rotate   to turn around a center point

The winds of a hurricane blow clockwise in the Southern Hemisphere and counterclockwise in the Northern Hemisphere. This picture taken from space shows the track of Hurricane Andrew, the most destructive U.S. hurricane on record.

Florida

Did You Know?

Hurricanes occur in the Atlantic, Caribbean, and eastern Pacific Oceans. In the western Pacific, severe tropical storms are called *typhoons*. In the Indian Ocean, they are known as *cyclones*.

It's Raining, It's Pouring

The wettest place in the United States is Mt. Waialeale (wy ah LAY ah LAY), on the island of Kauai in Hawaii. Over the last 30 years, Mt. Waialeale has received an annual average of 460 inches of rain! But on parts of the Kauai coast, only a few miles away, the rainfall is as little as 20 inches per year. Mt. Waialeale also holds the U.S. record for the greatest number of rainy days a year. It has up to 350 rainy days annually, with an average of 335 days!

Mt. Waialeale, Kauai, Hawaii

The driest place in the U.S. is Death Valley, California, which receives less than two inches of rain annually.

Altogether, how many feet of rain have fallen on Mt. Waialeale in the last 30 years? What is the average annual rainfall of Mawsynram (in feet and inches)?

World Records

- The wettest place in the world is Mawsynram, India, where the annual average rainfall is seven inches greater than at Mt. Waialeale.

- The driest place in the world is the Atacama Desert in northern Chile, where a total of one inch of rain has fallen in 100 years. Parts of the desert are thought to have gone without rain for 400 years.

Rainy Records

In the United States, the record rainfall for any 24-hour period is 43 inches. This huge amount of water fell in Alvin, Texas, on July 25 and 26, 1979. The map below shows the precipitation records for each of the other states. There are many other interesting rainfall records. For example, the fastest foot of rain ever recorded in the U.S. fell in just 42 minutes in Holt, Missouri, on June 22, 1947!

precipitation rain, snow, sleet, or hail

Record Maximum 24-Hour Precipitation (Inches)

UNITED STATES OF AMERICA

More Records

- The world-record rainfall for a 24-hour period is 74 inches. This rain fell on the island of Réunion on March 15 and 16, 1952.

- The highest one-year rainfall in the U.S. is 739 inches. This was recorded at Kuki, Hawaii, in the 12 months beginning December 1981.

- The world-record rainfall for a one-year period is 1,041 inches. This was recorded at Assam, India, from 1880 through 1881.

- During the longest dry spell in the U.S., no rain at all fell in Bagdad, California, from October 3, 1912, to November 8, 1914.

- At Arica in Chile's Atacama Desert, no rainfall was recorded for 14 years.

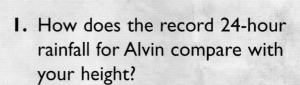

Figure It Out

How would you solve these problems?

1. How does the record 24-hour rainfall for Alvin compare with your height?

2. Suppose that the record-breaking rain in Holt had continued at the same rate.

   a. How many hours would it take for 10 feet of rain to fall?

   b. About how many feet of rain would fall in 24 hours?

3. Look at the map.

   a. Pick a state other than Texas. How much less than the record rainfall for Texas is the record for that state?

   b. Now pick two states. What is the difference between their 24-hour records?

4. For how many days did Bagdad's dry spell last?

Snowfall Statistics

Each year, an average of 105 snowstorms affect the
United States. A typical snowstorm lasts from two
to five days and brings snow to parts of several states.
The heaviest single snowstorm ever recorded was in 1959,
when 189 inches of snow fell in the Mt. Shasta Ski Bowl,
California, between February 13 and February 19.
Some other snowfall statistics for the U.S. are shown below.

Mt. Shasta

Greatest 24-Hour Snowfall

- 76 inches, April 14–15, 1921,
  Silver Lake, Colorado

Greatest One-Year Snowfall

- 1,122 inches, 1971–1972,
  Mount Rainier, Washington

Deepest Snow Cover

- 451 inches, March 11, 1911,
  Tamarack, California

Largest Snowflake

- 15 inches across,
  January 28, 1887,
  Fort Keogh, Montana

snow cover   a layer of snow on the surface of the ground

Snowfall is included in precipitation records. On average, 10 inches of snow is equivalent to one inch of rain. However, it can take anywhere from 5 inches of very wet snow to 15 inches of dry-powder snow to produce an inch of water.

Pick one of the record snowfalls on page 16. Find the equivalent amount of rain if the snow is—
• average.
• very wet.

Huge Hailstones

Hailstones cause about one billion dollars' worth of damage to crops and property every year in the United States. The record for the largest hailstone was set near Aurora, Nebraska, on June 22, 2003. This icy giant measured 7 inches across and $18\frac{3}{4}$ inches around. However, the heaviest hailstone on record fell in Coffeyville, Kansas, on September 3, 1970. It measured "only" $17\frac{1}{2}$ inches around, but it weighed about $1\frac{2}{3}$ pounds.

Hailstones can cause damage to cars and crops.

Use the graph to help you estimate the total number of large hail events in each month from April through June. What else can you tell from the graph?

This huge hailstone from Aurora has been preserved at the National Center for Atmospheric Research in Boulder, Colorado.

Size of Hailstones (by Month)

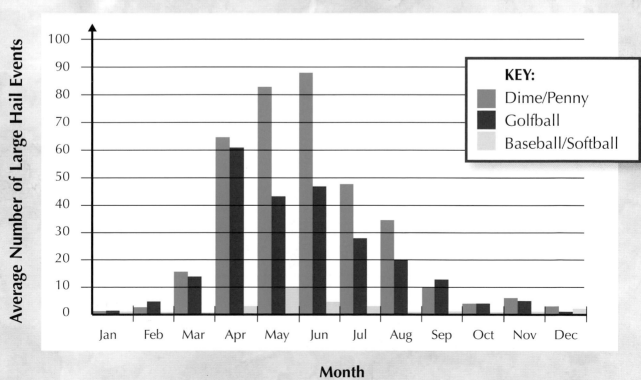

KEY:
- Dime/Penny
- Golfball
- Baseball/Softball

Average Number of Large Hail Events

Month

Highs and Lows

The highest temperature ever recorded in the United States was a scorching 134°F. This record was set at Greenland Ranch in Death Valley, California, on July 10, 1913. At the other end of the scale, the temperature at Prospect Creek, Alaska, plummeted to a record low of –79.8°F on January 23, 1971.

Record U.S. Monthly Maximum Temperatures		
Date	Place	Temperature
January 17, 1936	Laredo, Texas	98°F
February 3, 1963	Montezuma, Arizona	105°F
March 31, 1954	Rio Grande City, Texas	108°F
April 25, 1898	Volcano Springs, California	118°F
May 27, 1896	Salton, California	124°F
June 23, 1902	Volcano Springs, California	129°F
July 10, 1913	Greenland Ranch, California	134°F
August 12, 1933	Greenland Ranch, California	127°F
September 2, 1950	Mecca, California	126°F
October 5, 1917	Sentinel, Arizona	116°F
November 12, 1906	Craftonville, California	105°F
December 8, 1938	La Mesa, California	100°F

plummet   to drop suddenly

Make a Line Graph

To make a line graph that shows the record maximum temperature for each month, you will need a copy of the Blackline Master.

1. Write a heading for the graph. Also write J, F, M, … D to show the months.

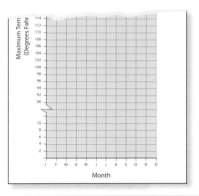

2. Plot a point on the graph to show the record temperature for January (on page 20).

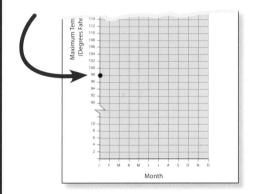

3. Plot points to show the record temperature for each of the other months.

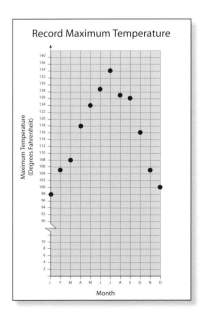

4. Draw lines to connect the points you plotted. (Use a ruler.)

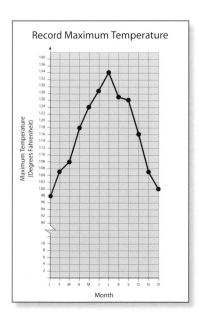

Record Changes

In the United States, the greatest difference in temperature during a 24-hour period occurred in Browning, Montana, from January 23 through 24, 1916. The maximum temperature during this time was 44°F, and the minimum temperature was –56°F! The most rapid temperature change in the U.S. may have occurred in Spearfish, South Dakota. On January 22, 1943, the temperature rose from –4°F at 7:30 A.M. to 45°F at 7:32 A.M.!

Use data from these pages to create two or three story problems. Then exchange your work with a partner and solve each other's problems.

When a heat wave hits, people are often drawn to water. During a massive heat wave in July 1940, thousands of New Yorkers flocked to Coney Island.

The world record for the longest heat wave was set in Marble Bar, Australia. The town recorded maximum daily temperatures greater than 100°F from October 30, 1923, through April 7, 1924.

Did You Know?

The rate at which tree crickets chirp is directly affected by the temperature. To estimate the temperature, count the number of chirps a cricket makes in 15 seconds and add 37.

Sample Answers

Find some weather data for your town or state. Make a graph, chart, or map to present the information you found.

Page 7   Texas

No, because it has a greater area than other tornado-prone states.

Page 13   1,150 ft; 38 ft, 11 in.

Page 15   2.   a. 7 hours

b. about $34\frac{1}{4}$ ft

4. 767 days (including both dates)

Page 17   76 inches: 7.6 inches,
15.2 inches;
451 inches: 45.1 inches,
90.2 inches;
1,122 inches: 112.2 inches,
224.4 inches

Page 19   April: 130; May: 136; June: 139

Index